Parables of Jesus for a Meaningful Life

Walking in the Master Teacher's Footsteps!

Gerard Assey

Parables of Jesus
for a Meaningful Life:
Walking in the
Master Teacher's Footsteps!

By
Gerard Assey

Published by:
Gerard Assey
19/18, Palli Arasan Street
Anna Nagar East
Chennai - 600 102

ISBN: 978-81-965807-4-2

(Image by vwalakte on Freepik @ www.Freepik.com
Thank you)

Table of Contents

- ✓ Preface
- ✓ Why Did Jesus Use Parables?
- ✓ Types of Parables and the Common Themes
- ✓ How to Use this Book Effectively

1. The Parable of the Sower (Matthew 13:3-23)
2. The Parable of the Weeds (Matthew 13:24-30)
3. The Parable of the Mustard Seed (Matthew 13:31-32)
4. The Parable of the Yeast (Matthew 13:33)
5. The Parable of the Hidden Treasure (Matthew 13:44)
6. The Parable of the Pearl of Great Price (Matthew 13:45-46)
7. The Parable of the Net (Matthew 13:47-50)
8. The Parable of the Unforgiving Servant (Matthew 18:21-35)
9. The Parable of the Lost Sheep (Matthew 18:12-14)
10. The Parable of the Good Samaritan (Luke 10:25-37)
11. The Parable of the Lost Coin (Luke 15:8-10)
12. The Parable of the Prodigal Son (Luke 15:11-32)
13. The Parable of the Good Shepherd (John 10:1-18)
14. The Parable of the Pharisee and the Tax Collector (Luke 18:9-14)

15. The Parable of the Wise and Foolish Builders (Matthew 7:24-27)
16. The Parable of the Two Sons (Matthew 21:28-32)
17. The Parable of the Wicked Tenants (Matthew 21:33-46)
18. The Parable of the Wedding Feast (Matthew 22:1-14)
19. The Parable of the Fig Tree (Luke 13:6-9)
20. The Parable of the Great Banquet (Luke 14:15-24)
21. The Parable of the Talents (Matthew 25:14-30)
22. The Parable of the Ten Virgins (Matthew 25:1-13)
23. The Parable of the Growing Seed (Mark 4:26-29)
24. The Parable of the Watchful Servants (Luke 12:35-40)
25. The Parable of the Moneylender (Luke 7:41-43)
26. The Parable of the Rich Fool (Luke 12:13-21)
27. The Parable of the Barren Fig Tree (Luke 13:6-9)
28. The Parable of the Unjust Judge (Luke 18:1-8)
29. The Parable of the Rich Man and Lazarus (Luke 16:19-31)
30. The Parable of the Pharisee and the Publican (Luke 18:9-14)
31. The Parable of the Leaven (Matthew 13:33)

32. The Parable of the Unfinished Tower (Luke 14:28-30)
33. The Parable of the Unfinished War (Luke 14:31-33)
34. The Parable of the Two Debtors (Luke 7:41-43)
35. The Parable of the Laborers in the Vineyard (Matthew 20:1-16)
36. The Parable of the Vine and Branches (John 15:1-8)
37. The Parable of the New Cloth (Matthew 9:16)
38. The Parable of the New Wine (Matthew 9:17)
39. The Parable of the Strong Man (Matthew 12:29)
40. The Parable of the Lamp on a Stand (Mark 4:21)

- ✓ Conclusion
- ✓ About the Author

Preface

In the timeless words of the Bible, we find a treasury of parables- profound stories told by Jesus Christ. These parables transcend the ages, carrying wisdom, insight, and guidance that resonate with people from all walks of life. They are more than stories; they are windows into the deepest dimensions of the human experience.

'Parables of Jesus for a Meaningful Life: *Walking in the Master Teacher's Footsteps!'* takes you on a journey through this extraordinary collection, each parable revealing a unique facet of truth, love, compassion, and the boundless grace of our Creator. These parables are an invitation to reflect, learn, and be inspired by the words of the one who uttered them more than two millennia ago.

As we delve into each parable, we discover more than just narratives. We unearth profound lessons, timeless principles, and an abiding message of hope. From the good Samaritan to the prodigal son, from the sower and the seed to the talents entrusted, each parable tells a story that reflects the human condition and points us toward a higher purpose.

This book is designed to be a guide, a source of inspiration, and a wellspring of understanding. For each parable, we present the relevant Bible verse, a detailed narration, points to reflect upon, key applications, and lessons for our lives. The goal is not just to understand the parables but to embrace their messages in our daily journey.

Whether you are seeking spiritual nourishment, guidance through life's challenges, or simply a deeper understanding of the teachings of Jesus,

‘Parables of Jesus for a Meaningful Life: *Walking in the Master Teacher’s Footsteps!’* welcomes you with open arms. It's a book that transcends religious boundaries and speaks to the universal quest for meaning and purpose.

May these parables illuminate your path, inspire your heart, and ignite your soul. Let them be a reminder that in the timeless wisdom of Christ, we find a beacon of light in a world that sometimes feels shadowed by uncertainty. The lessons contained within are as relevant today as they were when first spoken, and their impact is as profound as ever.

Prepare to embark on a transformative journey, exploring the wisdom of the ages and embracing the divine truths that have shaped the hearts and minds of countless individuals.

May this book be a source of enlightenment and enrichment as you discover the profound beauty of Jesus' parables and their relevance in our lives today, as you embark on a journey of reflection, learning, and spiritual growth.

Why Did Jesus Use Parables?

"He told them another parable: 'The kingdom of heaven is like a mustard seed, which a man took and planted in his field.'" — Matthew 13:31 (NIV)

The use of parables by Jesus is not merely a literary technique or a stylistic choice. It carries profound purpose and wisdom. Understanding why Jesus chose to convey His teachings through parables can deepen our appreciation of these timeless stories and shed light on their relevance in our lives today.

A Universal Language:

One of the key reasons Jesus used parables was to speak to a wide audience, transcending social, cultural, and educational boundaries. Parables are simple, relatable stories that anyone can understand, regardless of their background. By using everyday scenarios and relatable characters, Jesus ensured that His message would reach both the learned and the layperson.

Inviting Reflection:

Parables serve as mirrors reflecting our own lives, choices, and beliefs. They invite us to introspect and consider the moral and spiritual implications of our actions. In telling stories like the prodigal son or the good Samaritan, Jesus encouraged his listeners to put themselves in the shoes of the characters and ponder, "What would I do in that situation?" This reflection fosters spiritual growth and self-awareness.

Veiling Truth for the Sincere Seeker:

Interestingly, while parables are accessible to all, they also have a veiling effect. This was not to obscure the truth but to make it accessible to those who sincerely sought understanding. To those genuinely interested, the deeper meaning of a parable could be revealed, providing an opportunity for profound spiritual insight.

Engaging and Memorable:

A well-told story has a way of sticking in our memory. The use of parables ensured that the teachings of Jesus would be remembered and passed down through generations. This is precisely why these stories continue to be shared and cherished today.

Challenging Conventional Wisdom:

Parables often challenged conventional wisdom and the norms of the time. They encouraged listeners to think beyond societal norms, religious traditions, and stereotypes. By presenting a Samaritan as a hero in one parable or a tax collector as justified in another, Jesus provoked thought and pushed the boundaries of accepted beliefs.

An Ever-Relevant Message:

The beauty of parables is that their messages remain ever-relevant. Whether you're hearing these stories for the first time or the hundredth, they have the power to touch your heart and inspire you to live a life of greater compassion, love, and purpose.

In this book, we will explore 50 of these timeless parables. Each one has a unique message, but they all share the common thread of being spoken by a compassionate teacher who sought to awaken the hearts and minds of all who would listen.

As you journey through these parables, consider not only the lessons they offer but also the profound intention behind their use. May you find inspiration, understanding, and a deeper connection to the teachings of Jesus through these stories.

The parables are not just tales of the past; they are pathways to a brighter, more purposeful future.

Types of Parables and the Common Themes

Parables are a unique and powerful form of teaching used by Jesus to convey spiritual and moral lessons. They come in various types and often revolve around common themes. Let's explore the types and common themes of parables in detail:

Types of Parables:

- ✓ **Similitude Parables:** These parables begin with phrases like "the kingdom of heaven is like" or "the kingdom of God is like." They draw analogies between everyday situations or objects and spiritual truths. For example, the parable of the mustard seed (Matthew 13:31-32) compares the growth of God's kingdom to a tiny mustard seed that grows into a large tree.
- ✓ **Narrative Parables:** In these parables, Jesus tells a story with characters and events to illustrate a moral or spiritual lesson. For instance, the parable of the Good Samaritan (Luke 10:25-37) narrates a story of a compassionate Samaritan helping a wounded man, emphasizing the importance of loving one's neighbor.
- ✓ **Exemplar Parables:** These parables present individuals or characters who embody a particular trait or virtue. The parable of the Pharisee and the Tax Collector (Luke 18:9-14) exemplifies humility and righteousness through the contrasting prayers of the two characters.

- ✓ **Saying Parables:** These are shorter parables that convey a single lesson or idea. The parable of the new cloth and old garment (Matthew 9:16) or the parable of the new wine and old wineskins (Matthew 9:17) are examples. They emphasize the need for new ways of thinking and living.

Common Themes of Parables:

- ✓ **The Kingdom of God/Heaven:** Many parables revolve around the theme of the kingdom of God or the kingdom of heaven. They illustrate what this kingdom is like, how it grows, and how people enter it. The parable of the wheat and weeds (Matthew 13:24-30) speaks of the coexistence of good and evil until the final judgment.
- ✓ **Repentance and Forgiveness:** Numerous parables highlight the importance of repentance and God's willingness to forgive. The parable of the prodigal son (Luke 15:11-32) is a poignant illustration of a wayward son who repents and is warmly received by his father.
- ✓ **Mercy and Compassion:** Parables often emphasize the virtues of mercy and compassion. The parable of the Good Samaritan (Luke 10:25-37) and the parable of the unforgiving servant (Matthew 18:21-35) stress the need for forgiveness and compassionate action.
- ✓ **Humility and Righteousness:** The parable of the Pharisee and the Tax Collector (Luke 18:9-14) underscores the contrast between

self-righteousness and humility. It teaches the importance of a humble heart before God.

- ✓ **Persistence in Prayer and Faith:** The parable of the persistent widow (Luke 18:1-8) and the parable of the mustard seed (Matthew 13:31-32) highlight the power of persistence in prayer and the growth of faith from small beginnings.
- ✓ **Stewardship and Accountability:** Several parables address the responsibility of stewardship and accountability for one's actions. The parable of the talents (Matthew 25:14-30) speaks to the wise use of resources and gifts entrusted to us.
- ✓ **Inclusion and Reversal of Roles:** Parables like the parable of the great banquet (Luke 14:15-24) challenge societal norms and emphasize the inclusion of those who are often excluded. They depict a reversal of roles where the humble are exalted, and the proud are humbled.
- ✓ **Gratitude and Thankfulness:** The parable of the ten lepers (Luke 17:11-19) teaches the importance of gratitude. It underscores the significance of returning to express thankfulness for the blessings received.
- ✓ **Judgment and End Times:** Some parables deal with the final judgment and the end times. The parable of the sheep and goats (Matthew 25:31-46) illustrates the separation of the righteous and the unrighteous at the end of days.
- ✓ **Lost and Found:** Parables such as the parable of the lost sheep (Luke 15:3-7) and the parable of the lost coin (Luke 15:8-10)

convey the joy of recovery and restoration. They depict the seeking and finding of what was lost.

Understanding the types and themes of parables provides insight into the profound teachings of Jesus. These stories, with their rich symbolism and timeless lessons, continue to inspire and guide people on their spiritual journeys.

How to Use this Book Effectively

Using this book effectively to derive maximum benefit from the lessons it presents is essential. Here's a detailed guide for readers on how to make the most of the book and apply the teachings of the parables in their lives:

1. Begin with an Open Heart and Mind:

Approach the book with a willingness to learn and grow. Keep an open heart and mind to receive the wisdom these parables offer.

2. Read Mindfully:

Take your time when reading each parable. Reflect on the story and its characters. Imagine yourself in their shoes and immerse yourself in the narrative.

3. Meditate and Contemplate:

After reading a parable, spend some time in quiet reflection. Consider the message it conveys and how it relates to your life.

4. Journal Your Thoughts:

Maintain a journal as you read. Write down your insights, thoughts, and personal reflections for each parable. This practice can help you track your spiritual growth.

5. Connect with Others:

Share the parables and their teachings with friends, family, or a study group. Engaging in discussions can deepen your understanding and provide different perspectives.

6. Explore Related Scripture:

Often, the themes of the parables are connected to other biblical passages. Look up related verses and explore the broader context to gain a more comprehensive understanding.

7. Set Personal Goals:

After reading each parable, set personal goals or intentions based on the lessons learned. For example, if a parable emphasizes forgiveness, make it a goal to forgive someone in your life.

8. Apply the Lessons:

The key to benefiting from these parables is application. As you encounter challenges or opportunities in your daily life, think about how the lessons from the parables can guide your decisions and actions.

9. Practice Compassion and Kindness:

The parables often stress compassion, mercy, and love. Actively seek opportunities to show kindness and empathy to others, even in challenging circumstances.

10. Cultivate a Prayer and Meditation Routine:

Incorporate regular prayer and meditation into your daily routine. This can help you stay grounded and connected to the spiritual insights you gain from the parables.

11. Track Your Progress:

Periodically review your journal entries to see how you've applied the lessons over time. Celebrate your successes and identify areas for improvement.

12. Share Your Own Parables:

As you grow in your understanding of these parables, consider crafting your own stories to share with others. This can be a powerful way to pass on the wisdom you've gained.

13. Seek Guidance and Support:

If you encounter challenges in applying the lessons, don't hesitate to seek guidance from a spiritual mentor, counselor, or a trusted friend.

14. Be Patient with Yourself:

Personal growth is a journey, and it often involves setbacks and struggles. Be patient with yourself and continue to strive for improvement.

15. Revisit and Review:

Don't treat this book as a one-time read. Revisit the parables regularly. As you progress in your spiritual journey, you'll find new layers of meaning in the same stories.

16. Stay Grateful:

Gratitude is a recurring theme in many parables. Cultivate a mindset of thankfulness for the lessons you've learned and the growth you've experienced.

17. Extend the Lessons Beyond Yourself:

The teachings from these parables are not meant for personal gain alone. Look for ways to extend the lessons to benefit your community and society as a whole.

Incorporating these practices into your engagement with the book will help you derive maximum benefit from the parables and, more importantly, live out their teachings in your everyday life. Remember that spiritual growth is an ongoing process, and the wisdom of the parables can serve as a lifelong guide.

1. The Parable of the Sower

Bible Verse: Matthew 13:3-23 *"Then he told them many things in parables, saying: 'A farmer went out to sow his seed. As he was scattering the seed, some fell along the path, and the birds came and ate it up...'"*

Parable Narration: In this parable, Jesus speaks of a sower who goes out to sow seeds. The seeds fall on various types of soil. Some fall along the path and are eaten by birds, some fall on rocky ground and wither away, some fall among thorns and are choked, and some fall on good soil and produce a fruitful crop.

Points to Reflect On:

- ✓ The different types of soil represent the conditions of the human heart and how people receive and respond to the message of the kingdom.
- ✓ The rocky ground symbolizes those who receive the message with initial enthusiasm but fall away when faced with hardships or trials.
- ✓ The thorny ground represents those who hear the word but are consumed by the worries and distractions of the world.
- ✓ The good soil represents those who receive the word, understand it, and bear fruit.

Key Application: The Parable of the Sower teaches us that the effectiveness of God's Word in our lives depends on the condition of our hearts. It encourages us to prepare our hearts to receive

God's message, removing obstacles and distractions.

Lessons in Our Life:

- ✓ The Condition of the Heart: We should regularly examine the state of our hearts to ensure they are receptive to God's teachings. Removing hardness, rocky areas, and thorns in our hearts can lead to spiritual growth.
- ✓ Perseverance: This parable highlights the importance of perseverance in the face of trials and difficulties. We should not be discouraged by challenges but continue to nurture our faith.
- ✓ Fruitful Living: Just as good soil produces a harvest, a receptive heart can bear the fruit of good deeds, love, and spiritual growth. It reminds us that faith should lead to a transformed and fruitful life.

2. The Parable of the Weeds

Bible Verse: Matthew 13:24-30 *"Jesus told them another parable: 'The kingdom of heaven is like a man who sowed good seed in his field. But while everyone was sleeping, his enemy came and sowed weeds among the wheat, and went away...'"*

Parable Narration: In this parable, Jesus likens the kingdom of heaven to a man who sows good seed in his field. However, an enemy sows weeds among the wheat. When the wheat sprouts, so do the weeds. The man's servants propose pulling up the weeds, but he advises waiting until the harvest to avoid uprooting the wheat.

Points to Reflect On:

- ✓ The good seed represents the children of the kingdom, while the weeds symbolize the children of the evil one.
- ✓ The coexistence of wheat and weeds in the field mirrors the presence of both righteous and unrighteous people in the world.
- ✓ The decision to wait until the harvest illustrates God's patience and the final judgment when the righteous and the wicked will be separated.

Key Application: The Parable of the Weeds teaches us about the coexistence of good and evil in the world and the ultimate judgment by God. It reminds us of God's patience in allowing time for repentance and transformation.

Lessons in Our Life:

- ✓ Coexistence of Good and Evil: Just as the field contains both wheat and weeds, the world has both righteous and unrighteous individuals. This parable encourages us to show love and patience to all, recognizing that God is the ultimate judge.

- ✓ Avoid Hasty Judgment: The parable cautions against hasty judgment or attempts to uproot what we perceive as evil. We should trust in God's wisdom and timing for judgment.
- ✓ The Final Harvest: The parable emphasizes the reality of a final judgment. It encourages us to live righteously, knowing that in the end, the righteous will be gathered into God's kingdom, while the unrighteous will face judgment.

3. The Parable of the Mustard Seed

Bible Verse: Matthew 13:31-32 *"He told them another parable: 'The kingdom of heaven is like a mustard seed, which a man took and planted in his field. Though it is the smallest of all seeds, yet when it grows, it is the largest of garden plants and becomes a tree, so that the birds come and perch in its branches.'"*

Parable Narration: In this parable, Jesus compares the kingdom of heaven to a mustard seed, which is one of the smallest seeds. A man plants this tiny seed in his field, and although it starts small, it grows into a large tree, providing shelter for birds.

Points to Reflect On:

- ✓ The mustard seed symbolizes the small and seemingly insignificant beginnings of God's kingdom in the hearts of individuals.
- ✓ The remarkable growth of the mustard seed represents the expansion of God's kingdom as it impacts the lives of people and communities.
- ✓ The imagery of birds finding shelter in the mustard tree portrays the inclusive nature of God's kingdom, providing refuge and sustenance.

Key Application: The Parable of the Mustard Seed encourages us to have faith in the potential for significant growth and impact, even when our efforts or beginnings seem small. It illustrates the transformative power of God's kingdom in the world.

Lessons in Our Life:

- ✓ Faith in Small Beginnings: Just as the mustard seed begins as the smallest of seeds, we should have faith in the small steps we take in spreading God's message and love. Great things can result from humble beginnings.
- ✓ Kingdom Growth: The parable reminds us that God's kingdom can grow and impact the lives of many. It encourages us to actively participate in sharing the gospel and making a positive difference in the world.
- ✓ Inclusivity and Shelter: The image of birds finding shelter in the mustard tree represents the inclusive nature of God's kingdom. It teaches us to create an environment where all are welcome and can find refuge.

4. The Parable of the Yeast

Bible Verse: Matthew 13:33 *"He told them still another parable: 'The kingdom of heaven is like yeast that a woman took and mixed into about sixty pounds of flour until it worked all through the dough.'"*

Parable Narration: In this parable, Jesus compares the kingdom of heaven to the action of yeast. A woman takes a small amount of yeast and mixes it into a large quantity of flour until the yeast permeates all the dough.

Points to Reflect On:

- ✓ Yeast is often associated with growth and transformation. In this context, it symbolizes the pervasive influence of the kingdom of heaven in the lives of people and society.
- ✓ The process of mixing the yeast into the flour signifies the intentional and gradual spreading of God's message and principles.
- ✓ The parable emphasizes the transformative power of God's kingdom, which can bring about change from within.

Key Application: The Parable of the Yeast encourages us to understand the incremental and transformative nature of God's kingdom. It teaches us to be agents of positive change in the world by spreading the influence of God's love and truth.

Lessons in Our Life:

- ✓ Gradual Transformation: Just as yeast gradually works through the dough, God's kingdom often brings about change in people's lives over time. We should be patient with ourselves and others as we seek transformation.

- ✓ Influence through Intention: The parable highlights the intentional act of mixing the yeast. It reminds us of our role in sharing God's message and love with others, actively seeking to influence our surroundings for the better.
- ✓ Small Beginnings, Significant Impact: A small amount of yeast can affect a large amount of dough. Similarly, our efforts, no matter how modest they may seem, can have a significant impact when guided by faith and love.

5. The Parable of the Hidden Treasure

Bible Verse: Matthew 13:44 *"The kingdom of heaven is like treasure hidden in a field. When a man found it, he hid it again, and then in his joy went and sold all he had and bought that field."*

Parable Narration: In this parable, Jesus likens the kingdom of heaven to a hidden treasure in a field. A man discovers the treasure, buries it again to keep it a secret, and then joyfully sells all his possessions to purchase the entire field.

Points to Reflect On:

- ✓ The hidden treasure represents the value and significance of the kingdom of heaven, which is often not immediately apparent.
- ✓ The man's actions, selling all he has, demonstrate the depth of commitment and sacrifice required to obtain the treasure.
- ✓ The joy in his actions reflects the immeasurable worth and happiness found in experiencing God's kingdom.

Key Application: The Parable of the Hidden Treasure inspires us to recognize the priceless nature of God's kingdom and to be willing to make sacrifices and commit ourselves wholeheartedly to attain it.

Lessons in Our Life:

- ✓ Recognizing Value: Just as the man recognized the value of the hidden treasure, we should discern the immeasurable worth of God's kingdom and prioritize our pursuit of it.

- ✓ Wholehearted Commitment: The man's willingness to sell all he had demonstrates the need for wholehearted commitment to our faith. It challenges us to examine our own priorities and level of dedication.
- ✓ Joy in the Kingdom: The joy in the man's actions reminds us of the happiness found in a deep relationship with God. It encourages us to seek and treasure that joy above all else.

6. The Parable of the Pearl of Great Price

Bible Verse: Matthew 13:45-46 *"Again, the kingdom of heaven is like a merchant looking for fine pearls. When he found one of great value, he went away and sold everything he had and bought it."*

Parable Narration: In this parable, Jesus compares the kingdom of heaven to a merchant in search of fine pearls. When the merchant discovers a pearl of exceptional value, he willingly sells everything he owns to acquire it.

Points to Reflect On:

- ✓ The pearl of great value symbolizes the immeasurable worth and significance of God's kingdom.
- ✓ The merchant's decision to sell everything signifies the commitment and sacrifice required to obtain such a precious treasure.
- ✓ The pursuit of the pearl reflects the intentional and determined effort in seeking God's kingdom.

Key Application: The Parable of the Pearl of Great Price teaches us to recognize the supreme value of God's kingdom and the necessity of making profound sacrifices and commitments to attain it.

Lessons in Our Life:

- ✓ Valuing God's Kingdom: Just as the merchant recognized the worth of the valuable pearl, we should discern the incomparable value of God's kingdom in our lives and prioritize our pursuit of it.

- ✓ Total Commitment: The merchant's willingness to sell everything he owned exemplifies the need for complete devotion and readiness to let go of worldly attachments in our spiritual journey.
- ✓ Determination and Intention: The parable encourages us to be intentional and persistent in seeking God's kingdom, recognizing that it is worth all our efforts and sacrifices.

7. The Parable of the Net

Bible Verse: Matthew 13:47-50 *"Once again, the kingdom of heaven is like a net that was let down into the lake and caught all kinds of fish. When it was full, the fishermen pulled it up on the shore. Then they sat down and collected the good fish in baskets, but threw the bad away. This is how it will be at the end of the age. The angels will come and separate the wicked from the righteous and throw them into the blazing furnace, where there will be weeping and gnashing of teeth."*

Parable Narration: In this parable, Jesus describes the kingdom of heaven as a net cast into the lake to catch various types of fish. When the net is full, the fishermen pull it ashore and separate the good fish from the bad. The good fish are collected in baskets, while the bad fish are discarded.

Points to Reflect On:

- ✓ The net symbolizes the gathering of people into God's kingdom, bringing together individuals of all backgrounds and beliefs.
- ✓ The separation of the good and bad fish represents the final judgment at the end of the age, where the righteous will be distinguished from the wicked.
- ✓ The consequences of this judgment highlight the eternal fate of the wicked, who will face punishment.

Key Application: The Parable of the Net emphasizes the concept of a final judgment when the righteous and the wicked will be separated. It encourages us to live in alignment with God's principles and values, understanding the gravity of our choices.

Lessons in Our Life:

- ✓ Inclusivity of the Kingdom: The net's collection of various fish underscores the inclusivity of God's kingdom, which welcomes people from diverse backgrounds. It reminds us that God's grace is available to all.
- ✓ Final Judgment: The parable reminds us of the reality of a final judgment, where our actions and faith will have eternal consequences. It encourages us to live with a sense of accountability.
- ✓ Seeking Righteousness: The parable urges us to live righteously and align our lives with God's will, knowing that the righteous will be separated and rewarded, while the wicked will face judgment.

8. The Parable of the Unforgiving Servant

Bible Verse: Matthew 18:21-35 *"Then Peter came to Jesus and asked, 'Lord, how many times shall I forgive my brother or sister who sins against me? Up to seven times?' Jesus answered, 'I tell you, not seven times, but seventy-seven times...'"*

Parable Narration: In this parable, Jesus responds to Peter's question about forgiveness. He tells a story of a king who wished to settle accounts with his servants. One servant owed him an enormous debt that he could not repay. The servant begged for patience, and the king, moved with compassion, forgave the entire debt.

However, the forgiven servant encountered a fellow servant who owed him a much smaller sum. When the forgiven servant refused to show mercy and demanded payment, the fellow servant pleaded for patience, just as the forgiven servant had done with the king. Instead of showing the same mercy he had received, the forgiven servant had his fellow servant thrown into prison.

When the king learned of this, he was furious and had the unforgiving servant delivered to the jailers until he could repay the entire debt.

Points to Reflect On:

- ✓ The king represents God, who forgives our sins and debts, which we can never repay on our own.

- ✓ The forgiven servant's unwillingness to forgive the smaller debt symbolizes our failure to extend the same grace to others.
- ✓ The consequences faced by the unforgiving servant highlight the importance of showing mercy and forgiveness as a response to God's forgiveness.

Key Application: The Parable of the Unforgiving Servant teaches us the importance of extending forgiveness and mercy to others, just as we have received it from God. It underscores the notion that we should forgive because we have been forgiven.

Lessons in Our Life:

- ✓ God's Forgiveness: The parable emphasizes the boundless forgiveness God extends to us. We should remember this when dealing with the sins of others.
- ✓ Unforgiveness Harms Us: Refusing to forgive harms us more than it harms the one we refuse to forgive. It can lead to bitterness and estrangement from God's grace.
- ✓ Forgive as You've Been Forgiven: Just as we have received God's abundant forgiveness, we should offer the same forgiveness to others. This act of grace is central to our Christian faith and reflects God's love.

9. The Parable of the Lost Sheep

Bible Verse: Matthew 18:12-14 (NIV) *"What do you think? If a man owns a hundred sheep, and one of them wanders away, will he not leave the ninety-nine on the hills and go to look for the one that wandered off? And if he finds it, truly I tell you, he is happier about that one sheep than about the ninety-nine that did not wander off. In the same way, your Father in heaven is not willing that any of these little ones should perish."*

Parable Narration: In this parable, Jesus illustrates the kingdom of heaven by telling the story of a shepherd with a hundred sheep. When one of his sheep goes astray, the shepherd leaves the ninety-nine in the hills to search for the lost one. Once he finds the lost sheep, he rejoices more over it than the ninety-nine that remained.

Points to Reflect On:

- ✓ The lost sheep represents individuals who have strayed from God's path and are in need of redemption and guidance.
- ✓ The shepherd's willingness to leave the majority to seek the one lost sheep reflects God's relentless love and care for every individual.
- ✓ The joy and celebration upon finding the lost sheep highlight the joy in heaven over one sinner who repents.
- ✓ **Key Application:** The Parable of the Lost Sheep conveys the profound truth that God's love and mercy extend to those who have gone astray. It encourages us to seek and

bring back those who are lost in their faith or life.

Lessons in Our Life:

- ✓ God's Pursuit: This parable reminds us of God's relentless pursuit of those who have gone astray. We should be instruments of God's love, reaching out to those who are lost and in need of guidance.
- ✓ Value of Every Soul: The parable underscores the value of each individual in the eyes of God. It encourages us to treat every person with care and love, never giving up on anyone.
- ✓ Joy in Redemption: Just as there is joy in heaven over the return of a lost soul, there is great joy in helping others find their way back to God. It's a reminder of the importance of our role in this process.

10. The Parable of the Good Samaritan

Bible Verse: Luke 10:25-37 *"But he wanted to justify himself, so he asked Jesus, 'And who is my neighbor?' In reply, Jesus said: 'A man was going down from Jerusalem to Jericho when he was attacked by robbers...' "*

Parable Narration: In this parable, Jesus tells the story of a man who is traveling from Jerusalem to Jericho. Along the way, he is attacked by robbers who strip him of his clothing, beat him, and leave him for dead. A priest and a Levite both pass by the wounded man without offering any help. However, a Samaritan, who was typically regarded as an enemy by the Jews, takes pity on the man. He tends to his wounds, puts him on his donkey, and takes him to an inn, where he cares for him.

Points to Reflect On:

- ✓ The man who fell victim to the robbers represents human vulnerability and the suffering that can occur in life.
- ✓ The priest and Levite symbolize religious figures who fail to show compassion and love to their fellow humans.
- ✓ The Samaritan's actions reflect the importance of kindness, compassion, and mercy, even to those outside one's social or religious circle.

Key Application: The parable of the Good Samaritan reminds us that we should be willing to help those in need, regardless of their background or circumstances. It challenges us to break down prejudices and show love and compassion to all people.

Lessons in Our Life:

- ✓ Compassion and Action: This parable teaches us that it's not enough to feel compassion; we must also take action to help those in need. The Samaritan's actions demonstrate that true love is shown through deeds.
- ✓ Breaking Down Barriers: Jesus used a Samaritan, who was an outsider, as the hero of the story to emphasize that love knows no boundaries. We should be willing to help anyone, even those who may be considered our enemies.
- ✓ The Golden Rule: The parable embodies the essence of the Golden Rule, "Do unto others as you would have them do unto you." It challenges us to treat others with the same care and kindness we would want for ourselves.

11. The Parable of the Lost Coin

Bible Verse: Luke 15:8-10 *"Or suppose a woman has ten silver coins and loses one. Doesn't she light a lamp, sweep the house and search carefully until she finds it? And when she finds it, she calls her friends and neighbors together and says, 'Rejoice with me; I have found my lost coin.' In the same way, I tell you, there is rejoicing in the presence of the angels of God over one sinner who repents."*

Parable Narration: In this parable, Jesus speaks of a woman who has ten silver coins. She loses one of the coins and, determined to find it, she lights a lamp, sweeps the house, and searches diligently until she locates the lost coin. Overjoyed by her discovery, she calls her friends and neighbors to celebrate with her.

Points to Reflect On:

- ✓ The lost coin symbolizes individuals who have strayed from their faith or purpose and are in need of rediscovery.
- ✓ The woman's diligent search signifies the effort and determination required to find what is lost.
- ✓ The celebration with friends and neighbors emphasizes the joy in heaven over one sinner who repents.

Key Application: The Parable of the Lost Coin teaches us about the significance of seeking and finding those who are spiritually lost. It inspires us to actively search for and celebrate the return of those who have strayed.

Lessons in Our Life:

- ✓ Effort in Seeking the Lost: Just as the woman diligently searched for the lost coin, we should invest effort in seeking and guiding those who have lost their way in life or faith.
- ✓ Rejoicing in Redemption: The parable highlights the joy and celebration that accompany the return of what was lost. We should be filled with joy when people rediscover their faith or purpose.
- ✓ Value of Each Soul: Every individual is valuable in the eyes of God. This parable emphasizes the importance of actively reaching out to those who have strayed and welcoming them back into the fold.

12. The Parable of the Prodigal Son

Bible Verse: Luke 15:11-32 *"Jesus continued: 'There was a man who had two sons. The younger one said to his father, 'Father, give me my share of the estate.' So he divided his property between them...'"*

Parable Narration: In this parable, Jesus tells the story of a man with two sons. The younger son asks for his share of the inheritance and leaves for a distant country, where he squanders his wealth in reckless living. A famine strikes the land, and the young man finds himself impoverished and starving. He decides to return to his father and confesses his wrongdoing, hoping to be accepted as a hired servant.

Upon seeing his son from a distance, the father runs to him, embraces him, and orders a celebration to welcome him back. The older son, who remained obedient, becomes resentful. The father lovingly explains that they should rejoice because the lost son has returned.

Points to Reflect On:

- ✓ The younger son's rebellion and repentance illustrate the human journey of sin, self-discovery, and the desire to return to God.
- ✓ The father's unconditional love, forgiveness, and celebration reflect God's grace and mercy toward those who repent.
- ✓ The older son's resentment raises questions about self-righteousness and the need for a compassionate and forgiving attitude.

Key Application: The Parable of the Prodigal Son emphasizes the depth of God's love, forgiveness, and desire for reconciliation. It encourages us to repent and return to God, as well as to practice forgiveness and compassion toward others.

Lessons in Our Life:

- ✓ God's Unconditional Love: Just as the father in the parable demonstrates unconditional love and forgiveness, God's love is available to all who seek it through repentance.
- ✓ Repentance and Reconciliation: The younger son's story highlights the importance of repentance and the possibility of reconciliation with God, regardless of past mistakes.
- ✓ Avoiding Self-Righteousness: The older son's reaction reminds us to guard against self-righteousness and judgment. We should celebrate when others find their way back to God.
- ✓ Compassion and Forgiveness: The parable underscores the value of showing compassion and forgiveness to those who have strayed. We are called to extend grace as we have received it.

13.The Parable of the Good Shepherd

Bible Verse: John 10:1-18 *"I am the good shepherd. The good shepherd lays down his life for the sheep. The hired hand is not the shepherd and does not own the sheep. So when he sees the wolf coming, he abandons the sheep and runs away, and the wolf attacks the flock..."*

Parable Narration: In this parable, Jesus declares Himself as the good shepherd. He explains that the good shepherd cares for his sheep, knows them individually, and is willing to lay down his life to protect them. In contrast, a hired hand who does not own the sheep will flee when danger approaches, leaving the sheep vulnerable to harm.

Jesus continues by expressing His unique relationship with His followers, emphasizing that they know His voice, and He knows them by name. He underscores that He is the way to eternal life and that His mission is to provide abundant life for His sheep.

Points to Reflect On:

- ✓ Jesus as the good shepherd symbolizes His role as the protector, guide, and provider for His followers.
- ✓ The hired hand represents those who do not have a personal, sacrificial commitment to the well-being of the sheep.
- ✓ The concept of knowing and recognizing the shepherd's voice underscores the personal relationship Jesus has with His followers.

Key Application: The Parable of the Good Shepherd teaches us about Jesus' loving and sacrificial role as our protector and guide. It encourages us to trust Him and follow His voice in our spiritual journey.

Lessons in Our Life:

- ✓ Trust in Jesus: We are called to trust in Jesus as our good shepherd who protects and guides us in our spiritual journey.
- ✓ Personal Relationship: The parable emphasizes the importance of a personal and intimate relationship with Jesus, recognizing His voice and following His lead.
- ✓ Sacrificial Love: Just as the good shepherd is willing to lay down His life for the sheep, we should be willing to love and serve others sacrificially, following Jesus' example.
- ✓ Abundant Life: Jesus' promise of abundant life reminds us that following Him leads to spiritual fulfillment and purpose.

14. The Parable of the Pharisee and the Tax Collector

Bible Verse: Luke 18:9-14 *"To some who were confident of their own righteousness and looked down on everyone else, Jesus told this parable: 'Two men went up to the temple to pray, one a Pharisee and the other a tax collector...'"*

Parable Narration: In this parable, Jesus tells the story of two men who go to the temple to pray. One is a Pharisee, a religious leader known for his strict adherence to the law and perceived righteousness. The other is a tax collector, a profession often associated with corruption and sin.

The Pharisee prays with pride, boasting of his righteous deeds and expressing his contempt for others, especially the tax collector. In contrast, the tax collector stands at a distance, beating his chest, and humbly prays for God's mercy, acknowledging his own unworthiness.

Jesus concludes the parable by explaining that it was the tax collector, not the Pharisee, who went home justified before God, for "all those who exalt themselves will be humbled, and those who humble themselves will be exalted."

Points to Reflect On:

- ✓ The parable highlights the danger of self-righteousness and pride in religious practices.
- ✓ The contrast between the Pharisee's pride and the tax collector's humility underscores the importance of a humble heart in approaching God.

- ✓ Jesus' message focuses on God's grace, which is received through humility and repentance.

Key Application: The Parable of the Pharisee and the Tax Collector teaches us about the significance of humility in our relationship with God. It encourages us to approach God with a humble heart, recognizing our need for His mercy.

Lessons in Our Life:

- ✓ Beware of Self-Righteousness: The parable warns against self-righteousness and the tendency to judge others. We should examine our own hearts and attitudes in our religious practices.
- ✓ The Power of Humility: Humility is key to experiencing God's grace and mercy. We should approach God with a humble heart, acknowledging our need for His forgiveness.
- ✓ God's Perspective: The parable reminds us that God looks at the heart. It's not about our self-righteousness but our sincerity and humility in seeking a relationship with Him.
- ✓ Equality in God's Eyes: The parable reinforces the idea that all people, regardless of their background or past sins, have the opportunity to receive God's grace and be justified through humility and repentance.

15. The Parable of the Wise and Foolish Builders

Bible Verse: Matthew 7:24-27 *"Therefore everyone who hears these words of mine and puts them into practice is like a wise man who built his house on the rock. The rain came down, the streams rose, and the winds blew and beat against that house; yet it did not fall, because it had its foundation on the rock. But everyone who hears these words of mine and does not put them into practice is like a foolish man who built his house on sand. The rain came down, the streams rose, and the winds blew and beat against that house, and it fell with a great crash."*

Parable Narration: In this parable, Jesus tells the story of two builders. One is a wise builder who listens to His teachings and puts them into practice. He builds his house on a solid foundation of rock. The other is a foolish builder who hears Jesus' words but does not put them into practice. He constructs his house on a foundation of sand.

When a storm comes, the rain pours, the streams rise, and the winds blow, both houses face the same challenges. The house built on the rock stands firm, while the one built on the sand collapses with a great crash.

Points to Reflect On:

- ✓ The parable emphasizes the importance of not only hearing but also putting Jesus' teachings into practice.
- ✓ The foundation of the house represents the depth of one's faith and the life built upon it.

- ✓ The storm symbolizes the trials and challenges of life.

Key Application: The Parable of the Wise and Foolish Builders underscores the significance of building our lives on the solid foundation of God's Word and putting His teachings into practice. It encourages us to have a strong and resilient faith that can withstand the storms of life.

Lessons in Our Life:

- ✓ Action in Faith: It's not enough to hear God's Word; we must actively apply it in our lives. A living faith is one that manifests in our actions.
- ✓ Solid Foundation: Just as a house needs a strong foundation, our faith needs a strong foundation in God's Word. It provides stability and security in times of trouble.
- ✓ Challenges and Trials: The parable acknowledges that life comes with challenges and storms. Having a strong foundation in God's teachings helps us weather these difficulties.
- ✓ Wisdom and Foolishness: The distinction between the wise and foolish builders illustrates the outcomes of living a life based on faith and obedience versus one built on empty beliefs.

16. The Parable of the Two Sons

Bible Verse: Matthew 21:28-32 *"But what do you think? A man had two sons. He went to the first and said, 'Son, go and work today in the vineyard.' 'I will not,' he answered, but later he changed his mind and went. Then the father went to the other son and said the same thing. He answered, 'I will, sir,' but he did not go. Which of the two did what his father wanted?' 'The first,' they answered."*

Parable Narration: In this parable, Jesus tells the story of a father with two sons. The father instructs the first son to go and work in the vineyard. Initially, the son refuses, saying, "I will not." However, he later changes his mind and goes to work as instructed.

The father then approaches the second son and gives him the same directive. The second son responds with apparent willingness, saying, "I will, sir." However, he does not follow through and go to the vineyard.

Jesus asks those listening which of the two sons did what the father wanted, and they reply that it was the first son who initially refused but later obeyed.

Points to Reflect On:

- ✓ The parable contrasts outward words and actions with genuine obedience.
- ✓ The first son's change of heart and obedience illustrates the concept of repentance and transformation.
- ✓ The second son's superficial agreement without action represents hypocrisy and empty promises.

Key Application: The Parable of the Two Sons underscores the importance of genuine obedience and repentance in response to God's call. It encourages us to prioritize actions over mere words and appearances.

Lessons in Our Life:

- ✓ Repentance and Transformation: The first son's change of heart serves as a reminder that it's never too late to repent and turn towards obedience to God's will.
- ✓ Honesty over Hypocrisy: The second son's response highlights the danger of empty promises and hypocrisy. It encourages us to be honest in our commitments and follow through with our actions.
- ✓ Actions Speak Louder: The parable emphasizes the significance of our actions over our words. Our obedience to God's commands is more valuable than vocal agreement.
- ✓ The Value of Obedience: Genuine obedience to God's will is what truly matters in our faith journey. It's a reflection of our love and devotion to Him.

17. The Parable of the Wicked Tenants

Bible Verse: Matthew 21:33-46 *"Listen to another parable: There was a landowner who planted a vineyard. He put a wall around it, dug a winepress in it and built a watchtower. Then he rented the vineyard to some farmers and moved to another place..."*

Parable Narration: In this parable, Jesus describes a landowner who planted a vineyard. He took great care to ensure the vineyard's success, building a protective wall around it, digging a winepress, and constructing a watchtower. The landowner then entrusted the vineyard to tenant farmers and moved to another place.

When it was time for the harvest, the landowner sent his servants to collect the fruit. However, the tenants mistreated and killed the servants. The landowner sent more servants, but the tenants treated them the same way. Finally, the landowner decided to send his son, thinking that the tenants would respect him.

But when the tenants saw the landowner's son, they conspired to seize the inheritance and killed him, hoping to take possession of the vineyard. Jesus then asks the crowd what the landowner will do to the wicked tenants. The people respond that the landowner will bring them to a wretched end and give the vineyard to other tenants who will produce fruit for him.

Points to Reflect On:

- ✓ The vineyard represents God's people and the blessings He bestows upon them.

- ✓ The tenant farmers symbolize religious leaders and those responsible for caring for God's people.
- ✓ The rejection and mistreatment of the landowner's servants and son reflect the rejection of God's messengers, including Jesus, by those entrusted with spiritual leadership.
- ✓ Key Application: The Parable of the Wicked Tenants emphasizes the responsibility of religious leaders and individuals to produce spiritual fruit and care for God's people. It warns against the consequences of rejecting God's messengers and the inheritance of His kingdom.

Lessons in Our Life:

- ✓ Responsibility for Spiritual Fruit: We are called to produce spiritual fruit and take care of the blessings and responsibilities God has entrusted to us, including nurturing our faith and sharing it with others.
- ✓ Rejection of God's Messengers: The parable serves as a cautionary tale about the consequences of rejecting God's messengers and failing to heed their messages.
- ✓ Justice and Accountability: God is just and holds individuals accountable for their actions. The parable reminds us that our choices have consequences.
- ✓ Caring for God's People: We should be diligent and faithful in caring for the spiritual well-being of God's people, promoting love, justice, and righteousness.

18. The Parable of the Wedding Feast

Bible Verse: Matthew 22:1-14 *"Jesus spoke to them again in parables, saying: 'The kingdom of heaven is like a king who prepared a wedding banquet for his son...'"*

Parable Narration: In this parable, Jesus tells the story of a king who arranges a grand wedding feast for his son. He sends out his servants to invite those who were originally on the guest list, but they refuse to come. Undeterred, the king sends more servants with a message that the banquet is ready, and he has prepared a lavish feast.

However, the invited guests continue to make excuses and decline the invitation. Some even mistreat the king's servants. In response to their refusal, the king opens the invitation to anyone they can find, both good and bad, so that the wedding hall is filled with guests.

The king enters the banquet to greet the guests but notices a man who is not dressed in wedding attire. The king asks the man how he entered without the proper clothing, but the man remains speechless. The king orders his attendants to bind the man hand and foot and throw him outside, where there will be weeping and gnashing of teeth.

Points to Reflect On:

- ✓ The king represents God, and the wedding feast symbolizes the invitation to enter His kingdom.

- ✓ The originally invited guests symbolize those who were first offered the opportunity to accept God's invitation but rejected it.
- ✓ The man without wedding attire signifies the importance of being spiritually prepared and clothed in righteousness.

Key Application: The Parable of the Wedding Feast highlights the urgency of accepting God's invitation to His kingdom and the necessity of being spiritually prepared. It teaches us the significance of responding to God's call with sincerity and reverence.

Lessons in Our Life:

- ✓ Accepting God's Invitation: We are urged to respond to God's call and invitation to His kingdom with gratitude and eagerness.
- ✓ The Open Invitation: God's invitation is extended to all, regardless of background or past sins. It emphasizes the inclusivity of His grace.
- ✓ Spiritual Preparation: Just as the wedding guests were expected to wear appropriate attire, we should be spiritually prepared, clothed in righteousness, and living in alignment with God's will.
- ✓ Accountability: The parable underscores the importance of accountability and readiness for God's judgment. It reminds us of the consequences of neglecting the call to His kingdom.

19. The Parable of the Fig Tree

Bible Verse: Luke 13:6-9 *"Then he told this parable: 'A man had a fig tree growing in his vineyard, and he went to look for fruit on it but did not find any. So he said to the man who took care of the vineyard, 'For three years now I've been coming to look for fruit on this fig tree and haven't found any. Cut it down! Why should it use up the soil?' 'Sir,' the man replied, 'leave it alone for one more year, and I'll dig around it and fertilize it. If it bears fruit next year, fine! If not, then cut it down.'"*

Parable Narration: In this parable, Jesus describes a man who has a fig tree growing in his vineyard. For three years, he has been searching for fruit on the tree but has found none. Frustrated, he instructs the vineyard keeper to cut down the unproductive tree since it's occupying space without bearing fruit.

However, the vineyard keeper pleads with the owner, requesting one more year to give the tree special attention. He promises to dig around the tree's roots and fertilize it. If, after this extra care, the tree still does not bear fruit, then it can be cut down.

Points to Reflect On:

- ✓ The fig tree represents individuals or groups that have the potential for spiritual growth and fruitfulness.
- ✓ The owner's patience and the vineyard keeper's efforts demonstrate God's mercy and willingness to provide opportunities for repentance and transformation.

- ✓ The need for fruitfulness symbolizes the importance of living a life aligned with God's will and producing good works.

Key Application: The Parable of the Fig Tree teaches us about God's patience, mercy, and His desire for spiritual growth and fruitfulness. It encourages us to seize the opportunity for repentance and bearing good fruit in our lives.

Lessons in Our Life:

- ✓ God's Patience: The parable reminds us of God's patience with us. He provides opportunities for us to bear fruit and grow spiritually.
- ✓ Opportunity for Repentance: We should recognize the grace and time God gives us to turn our lives around and become more fruitful in our faith and actions.
- ✓ Spiritual Growth: The fig tree's potential for growth underscores our potential for spiritual growth and the importance of continually drawing nourishment from God's Word.
- ✓ Fruitful Living: The parable encourages us to bear fruit in the form of good works, love, and positive impact on others, in accordance with God's will.

20. The Parable of the Great Banquet

Bible Verse: Luke 14:15-24 *"When one of those at the table with him heard this, he said to Jesus, 'Blessed is the one who will eat at the feast in the kingdom of God.' Jesus replied: 'A certain man was preparing a great banquet and invited many guests...'"*

Parable Narration: In this parable, Jesus tells the story of a man who is preparing a great banquet. The host sends out invitations to many guests, and when the time for the banquet arrives, he sends his servant to let the guests know that everything is ready. However, one by one, the invited guests make excuses and decline to attend.

The host becomes angry and instructs his servant to go out into the streets and alleys of the town to bring in the poor, the crippled, the blind, and the lame, so that the banquet hall may be filled. Even after doing so, there is still room, so the host commands the servant to go to the highways and hedges and compel people to come in so that his house will be full. He declares that none of the originally invited guests will taste his banquet.

Points to Reflect On:

- ✓ The great banquet represents the invitation to God's kingdom and the blessings of eternal life.
- ✓ The invited guests symbolize those who were given the opportunity to accept God's invitation but made excuses and rejected it.
- ✓ The poor, crippled, blind, and lame represent those who might be considered outsiders or

marginalized but are welcomed into God's kingdom.

Key Application: The Parable of the Great Banquet emphasizes the availability of God's invitation to His kingdom to all, regardless of their social status, and the consequences of rejecting that invitation. It encourages us to accept the invitation with gratitude and respond to God's call.

Lessons in Our Life:

- ✓ Accepting God's Invitation: We should be eager to accept God's invitation to His kingdom and partake in the blessings He offers.
- ✓ Inclusivity of God's Grace: God's invitation extends to all, regardless of their background, status, or past. His grace is inclusive and not limited to a select few.
- ✓ Consequences of Rejection: The parable underscores the consequences of rejecting God's invitation. Those who refuse will miss out on the blessings of His kingdom.
- ✓ Compelling Others: We are encouraged to share the good news of God's invitation with others, even those who may not initially seem interested or deserving.

21. The Parable of the Talents

Bible Verse: Matthew 25:14-30 *"Again, it will be like a man going on a journey, who called his servants and entrusted his wealth to them. To one he gave five bags of gold, to another two bags, and to another one bag, each according to his ability. Then he went on his journey..."*

Parable Narration: In this parable, Jesus describes a man who is about to go on a journey. Before leaving, he entrusts his wealth to his servants. To one servant, he gives five bags of gold, to another two bags, and to a third one bag, each according to their abilities.

The servant who received five bags of gold immediately goes out, invests the money, and earns an additional five bags. The servant with two bags also invests wisely and doubles his amount. However, the servant who received one bag buries it in the ground, fearing the master's judgment.

After a long time, the master returns and settles accounts with his servants. He praises the first two servants for their faithfulness and wise investment, and he rewards them with greater responsibilities. However, the third servant, who buried the one bag of gold, is rebuked for his fear and lack of initiative. The master takes the one bag from him and gives it to the first servant, casting the unfaithful servant into the darkness.

Points to Reflect On:

The bags of gold represent the resources, talents, and blessings that God entrusts to each individual.

The parable underscores the importance of stewardship and using one's abilities and resources for God's purposes.

The consequences for the third servant illustrate the accountability we have for how we manage what God has given us.

Key Application: The Parable of the Talents teaches us about the responsibility of using our God-given resources, abilities, and opportunities wisely and for His glory. It encourages us to be faithful stewards and to invest in God's kingdom.

Lessons in Our Life:

- ✓ Stewardship: We are called to be faithful stewards of the resources, talents, and opportunities God has given us. Our faithfulness in small things reflects our trustworthiness for greater responsibilities.
- ✓ Risk and Initiative: The first two servants took risks and initiative to invest their talents. The parable encourages us to take bold steps for God's kingdom and not to let fear hold us back.
- ✓ Accountability: The parable emphasizes our accountability to God for how we use our gifts and blessings. It reminds us that we will one day give an account of our stewardship.
- ✓ Reward and Consequences: Faithfulness is rewarded, while negligence has consequences. The parable teaches us that God honors those who use their talents for His purposes.

22. The Parable of the Ten Virgins

Bible Verse: Matthew 25:1-13 *"At that time, the kingdom of heaven will be like ten virgins who took their lamps and went out to meet the bridegroom..."*

Parable Narration: In this parable, Jesus describes ten virgins who are awaiting the arrival of the bridegroom for a wedding feast. They take their lamps and go out to meet him. Five of the virgins are wise, bringing extra oil for their lamps, while the other five are foolish, carrying lamps without any extra oil.

As they wait, the bridegroom is delayed, and all ten virgins become drowsy and fall asleep. At midnight, a cry goes out that the bridegroom is coming. The virgins rise to trim their lamps, but the foolish ones realize that their lamps are running out of oil. They ask the wise virgins for oil, but they are told to go buy more oil for themselves.

While the foolish virgins are away purchasing oil, the bridegroom arrives. The wise virgins go in with him to the wedding feast, and the door is shut. Later, the foolish virgins return, knocking on the door, but they are not allowed in. The bridegroom tells them, "I don't know you."

Points to Reflect On:

- ✓ The virgins represent individuals who are awaiting the return of Jesus and the establishment of His kingdom.
- ✓ The lamps symbolize faith and readiness, while the oil represents the Holy Spirit and spiritual preparedness.

- ✓ The parable illustrates the importance of being spiritually prepared for Christ's return and not relying on the preparedness of others.

Key Application: The Parable of the Ten Virgins emphasizes the need for personal spiritual readiness, preparedness for Christ's return, and the indwelling of the Holy Spirit. It encourages us to be vigilant and prepared for the unexpected return of Christ.

Lessons in Our Life:

- ✓ Personal Preparedness: We must individually ensure our spiritual readiness and not rely on the faith of others. Our relationship with God is a personal responsibility.
- ✓ The Holy Spirit: The parable highlights the significance of having the Holy Spirit dwelling within us. It is the oil that keeps our lamps burning and our faith alive.
- ✓ Readiness for Christ's Return: We are reminded to be vigilant and ready for Christ's return, as it can happen when we least expect it.
- ✓ The Consequence of Unpreparedness: The parable teaches us the consequences of spiritual unpreparedness when it is too late to make amends.

23. The Parable of the Growing Seed

Bible Verse: Mark 4:26-29 *"He also said, 'This is what the kingdom of God is like. A man scatters seed on the ground. Night and day, whether he sleeps or gets up, the seed sprouts and grows, though he does not know how. All by itself, the soil produces grain—first the stalk, then the head, then the full kernel in the head. As soon as the grain is ripe, he puts the sickle to it because the harvest has come.'"*

Parable Narration: In this parable, Jesus describes the kingdom of God using the analogy of a man who scatters seed on the ground. The man's actions represent the sowing of God's Word and the message of the kingdom. Day and night, whether the man sleeps or is awake, the seed begins to sprout and grow in the soil, without the man fully understanding the process.

The growth happens automatically, as if the earth produces the grain by itself. The growth follows a natural progression—first the stalk, then the head, and finally the full kernel in the head. When the grain is ripe and ready for harvest, the man wields the sickle to collect the crop because the time for harvesting has arrived.

Points to Reflect On:

- ✓ The seed represents God's Word and the message of the kingdom.
- ✓ The parable emphasizes the organic and mysterious growth of God's Word in the hearts of people.

- ✓ The readiness of the harvest signifies the appointed time for the culmination of God's work.

Key Application: The Parable of the Growing Seed illustrates the organic and transformative power of God's Word and the message of the kingdom in people's lives. It encourages us to sow the seeds of faith and trust in the divine process, understanding that growth and fruitfulness are God's work.

Lessons in Our Life:

- ✓ Sowing God's Word: We are called to share God's Word and the message of the kingdom with others, trusting that it has the power to take root and grow in their hearts.
- ✓ Divine Work: The parable reminds us that the growth and transformation of individuals are not solely our efforts but the work of God's Spirit. We should trust the process.
- ✓ Mystery of Growth: Like the farmer who doesn't fully comprehend the growth of the seed, we may not always understand how God is working in people's lives, but we can have faith that He is at work.
- ✓ Appointed Time: The parable teaches us that there is an appointed time for the culmination of God's work, signifying the ripeness of hearts for acceptance and transformation.

24. The Parable of the Watchful Servants

Bible Verse: Luke 12:35-40 *"Be dressed ready for service and keep your lamps burning, like servants waiting for their master to return from a wedding banquet, so that when he comes and knocks, they can immediately open the door for him. It will be good for those servants whose master finds them watching when he comes..."*

Parable Narration: In this parable, Jesus describes a master who instructs his servants to be dressed and ready for service, with their lamps burning, as they await his return from a wedding banquet. The master's return time is uncertain, and he wants his servants to be prepared for his arrival.

The key emphasis is on being watchful and ready for the master's return. The master assures the servants that when he finds them watchful and ready to open the door immediately upon his arrival, he will reward them.

Points to Reflect On:

- ✓ The master symbolizes Jesus, and the servants represent His followers who are awaiting His return.
- ✓ The parable stresses the importance of readiness, vigilance, and faithfulness in the anticipation of Christ's return.
- ✓ The uncertainty of the master's return underscores the unpredictable nature of Christ's return.

Key Application: The Parable of the Watchful Servants teaches us about the significance of being spiritually prepared, watchful, and faithful while awaiting the return of Christ. It encourages us to live in anticipation of His coming and to be ready to welcome Him with open hearts.

Lessons in Our Life:

- ✓ Spiritual Preparedness: We are reminded of the importance of being spiritually prepared and watchful for Christ's return, as it can happen at any moment.
- ✓ Vigilance and Faithfulness: We should maintain our faith and commitment to Christ, continuing to live in accordance with His teachings.
- ✓ Uncertainty of His Return: The parable emphasizes that the exact timing of Christ's return is unknown, and we should be continually watchful, not complacent.
- ✓ Reward for Faithfulness: Those who remain faithful and watchful will be rewarded by Christ when He returns.

25. The Parable of the Moneylender

Bible Verse: Luke 7:41-43 *"Two people owed money to a certain moneylender. One owed him five hundred denarii, and the other fifty. Neither of them had the money to pay him back, so he forgave the debts of both. Now which of them will love him more?"*

Parable Narration: In this parable, Jesus tells the story of a moneylender who is owed money by two individuals. One person owes a significant amount, specifically five hundred denarii, while the other owes a smaller amount of fifty denarii. Both debtors are unable to repay the moneylender, and, in an act of mercy and forgiveness, he decides to forgive the debts of both individuals.

Jesus then poses a question to his listeners, asking which of the debtors will love the moneylender more.

Points to Reflect On:

- ✓ The moneylender represents God, and the debt symbolizes the sins and wrongdoing of the two individuals.
- ✓ The parable highlights the contrast between the depth of forgiveness and the response of gratitude and love.
- ✓ It underscores the idea that those who have been forgiven more tend to love and appreciate the forgiver to a greater extent.

Key Application: The Parable of the Moneylender emphasizes the profound nature of God's forgiveness and the idea that those who recognize the extent of their forgiveness are more likely to respond with love and gratitude. It encourages us to acknowledge the depth of God's forgiveness in our lives.

Lessons in Our Life:

- ✓ God's Forgiveness: We should recognize the vastness of God's forgiveness for our sins and wrongdoings. God's mercy and forgiveness are boundless.
- ✓ Gratitude and Love: The parable teaches us that understanding the depth of God's forgiveness can lead to a deeper sense of gratitude and love for Him.
- ✓ Comparison and Humility: The parable reminds us not to compare ourselves with others in terms of sin but to humbly acknowledge our own need for forgiveness.
- ✓ The Transformative Power of Forgiveness: Experiencing and understanding God's forgiveness can lead to transformed lives and a desire to live in accordance with His will.

26. The Parable of the Rich Fool

Bible Verse: Luke 12:13-21 *"Someone in the crowd said to him, 'Teacher, tell my brother to divide the inheritance with me.' Jesus replied, 'Man, who appointed me a judge or an arbiter between you?' Then he said to them, 'Watch out! Be on your guard against all kinds of greed; life does not consist in an abundance of possessions.' And he told them this parable: 'The ground of a certain rich man yielded an abundant harvest...'"*

Parable Narration: In this parable, a man in the crowd approaches Jesus, seeking His intervention in a dispute over the division of an inheritance. Instead of directly addressing the dispute, Jesus warns the crowd about the dangers of greed and the desire for wealth.

He proceeds to tell the parable of a rich man whose land yields a bountiful harvest. The man decides to tear down his old barns and build bigger ones to store his surplus grain and goods. He plans to relax, eat, drink, and be merry, thinking that he has secured his future. However, God admonishes him, saying, "You fool! This very night your life will be demanded from you. Then who will get what you have prepared for yourself?"

Points to Reflect On:

- ✓ The parable highlights the folly of placing primary value on material wealth and possessions.
- ✓ It emphasizes the transient nature of life and the uncertainty of one's future.

- ✓ The parable serves as a warning against greed and the pursuit of earthly treasures at the expense of spiritual priorities.

Key Application: The Parable of the Rich Fool serves as a powerful reminder to prioritize eternal and spiritual matters over the accumulation of material wealth. It encourages us to guard against greed and focus on values and treasures that have lasting significance.

Lessons in Our Life:

- ✓ Prioritizing Spiritual Wealth: The parable teaches us to prioritize spiritual wealth and the values of God's kingdom over material possessions, which are temporary.
- ✓ Uncertainty of Life: We are reminded of the unpredictability of life and the importance of being prepared for the eternal rather than just the temporal.
- ✓ Greed and Contentment: The parable warns against the destructive nature of greed and encourages contentment with what we have.
- ✓ Investing in Eternal Treasures: We should invest in acts of love, kindness, and service that have eternal value rather than hoarding wealth for self-indulgence.

27. The Parable of the Barren Fig Tree

Bible Verse: Luke 13:6-9 *"Then he told this parable: 'A man had a fig tree growing in his vineyard, and he went to look for fruit on it but did not find any. So he said to the man who took care of the vineyard, "For three years now I've been coming to look for fruit on this fig tree and haven't found any. Cut it down! Why should it use up the soil?"'"*

Parable Narration: In this parable, Jesus describes a man who owns a fig tree growing in his vineyard. The man goes to check the tree for fruit but finds none. He's been coming for three years, expecting it to bear fruit, but it remains barren. Frustrated, he instructs the caretaker of the vineyard to cut the fig tree down since it's using up the soil without producing fruit.

However, the caretaker pleads for another chance and suggests that he will dig around the tree and fertilize it. If it bears fruit the following year, well and good; if not, then it can be cut down.

Points to Reflect On:

- ✓ The fig tree represents individuals or communities who, despite receiving God's care and attention, have not produced the expected fruits of righteousness and goodness.
- ✓ The parable highlights God's patience and willingness to grant additional time for repentance and transformation.

- ✓ It underscores the need for productivity and fruitfulness in response to God's grace and care.

Key Application: The Parable of the Barren Fig Tree calls us to recognize the importance of bearing fruit in our lives, responding to God's grace, and not wasting the opportunities and resources provided to us. It also underscores God's patience and desire for our repentance and spiritual growth.

Lessons in Our Life:

- ✓ Bearing Fruit: We are called to produce the fruits of righteousness, love, and good deeds in response to God's grace and care.
- ✓ God's Patience: The parable highlights God's patience and willingness to grant us time for repentance and transformation. It's a reminder of His abundant mercy.
- ✓ Opportunity for Change: We should seize the opportunity for spiritual growth and change, as well as make the most of the resources and care provided by God.
- ✓ Accountability: The parable reminds us of our accountability for the resources and opportunities we have received and the need to use them for the kingdom's work.

28. The Parable of the Unjust Judge/ Persistent Widow

Bible Verse: Luke 18:1-8 *"Then Jesus told his disciples a parable to show them that they should always pray and not give up. He said: 'In a certain town, there was a judge who neither feared God nor cared what people thought. And there was a widow in that town who kept coming to him with the plea, "Grant me justice against my adversary." For some time, he refused. But finally, he said to himself, "Even though I don't fear God or care what people think, yet because this widow keeps bothering me, I will see that she gets justice, so that she won't eventually come and attack me!"' And the Lord said, 'Listen to what the unjust judge says. And will not God bring about justice for his chosen ones, who cry out to him day and night? Will he keep putting them off? I tell you, he will see that they get justice and quickly. However, when the Son of Man comes, will he find faith on the earth?'"*

Parable Narration: In this parable, Jesus tells the story of an unjust judge in a certain town who neither feared God nor cared about people's opinions. In the same town, there was a persistent widow who repeatedly approached the judge with a plea for justice against her adversary. Initially, the judge refused to grant her request. However, because of her unrelenting persistence, he eventually decided to grant her justice, fearing that she might wear him down with her persistence.

Jesus uses this parable to illustrate the importance of persistent and unwavering prayer. He emphasizes that if an unjust judge would eventually respond to persistent pleas, how much more will God, who is just and compassionate, bring about justice for His chosen ones who cry out to Him day and night.

Points to Reflect On:

- ✓ The unjust judge represents a contrast to God, emphasizing the importance of God's justice and compassion.
- ✓ The widow symbolizes the persistence and faith of believers in their prayers to God.
- ✓ The parable encourages unwavering faith in prayer and the certainty of God's justice.

Key Application: The Parable of the Unjust Judge underscores the significance of persistent and unwavering prayer. It calls us to trust in God's justice, remain steadfast in our prayers, and not lose heart.

Lessons in Our Life:

- ✓ Persistent Prayer: We are encouraged to maintain a spirit of persistent and unwavering prayer, knowing that God hears our pleas and responds in His perfect timing.
- ✓ Trusting in God's Justice: The parable reminds us of God's justice and compassion. We can trust that He will bring about justice for His chosen ones.
- ✓ Avoiding Despair: It encourages us not to lose heart but to persevere in our prayers, even in challenging times.
- ✓ Maintaining Faith: The parable challenges us to maintain our faith and trust in God's ability to answer our prayers.

29. The Parable of the Rich Man and Lazarus

Bible Verse: Luke 16:19-31 *"There was a rich man who was dressed in purple and fine linen and lived in luxury every day. At his gate was laid a beggar named Lazarus, covered with sores and longing to eat what fell from the rich man's table. Even the dogs came and licked his sores. The time came when the beggar died and the angels carried him to Abraham's side. The rich man also died and was buried. In Hades, where he was in torment, he looked up and saw Abraham far away, with Lazarus by his side. So he called to him, 'Father Abraham, have pity on me and send Lazarus to dip the tip of his finger in water and cool my tongue because I am in agony in this fire.'"*

Parable Narration: In this parable, Jesus contrasts the lives of two individuals: a wealthy man who dressed in luxury and a beggar named Lazarus who was laid at the rich man's gate, covered in sores, and longing for scraps from the rich man's table. Even the dogs showed more compassion by licking Lazarus's sores.

Both the rich man and Lazarus died. Lazarus was carried by angels to be with Abraham, signifying his place in heaven, while the rich man ended up in Hades, experiencing torment. He saw Lazarus with Abraham and called out, requesting relief from his suffering. He asked Abraham to send Lazarus to cool his tongue with a drop of water, but Abraham explained that there was an unbridgeable chasm between them.

The rich man then asked Abraham to send Lazarus to warn his family to avoid the same fate. Abraham responded that they have Moses and the prophets, and if they do not listen to them, they would not be convinced even if someone rose from the dead.

Points to Reflect On:

- ✓ The parable illustrates the stark contrast between the rich man's luxurious life and Lazarus's suffering.
- ✓ It emphasizes the importance of compassion and caring for the less fortunate.
- ✓ The parable highlights the eternal consequences of one's actions and the significance of responding to God's message.

Key Application: "The Parable of the Rich Man and Lazarus" serves as a warning about the consequences of a self-indulgent and uncompassionate life. It also emphasizes the need to heed God's message and respond to His call.

Lessons in Our Life:

- ✓ Compassion and Generosity: The parable challenges us to show compassion and generosity to those in need, recognizing the value of caring for others.
- ✓ Eternal Consequences: It reminds us of the eternal consequences of our actions and choices, urging us to live in accordance with God's principles.
- ✓ Responsiveness to God's Message: We are encouraged to pay heed to God's message as revealed through Scripture and spiritual teachings, as ignoring it can lead to spiritual poverty.
- ✓ A Call to Repentance: The parable underscores the urgency of repentance and

responding to God's call while we have the opportunity to do so.

30. The Parable of the Pharisee and the Publican

Bible Verse: Luke 18:9-14 *"To some who were confident of their own righteousness and looked down on everyone else, Jesus told this parable: 'Two men went up to the temple to pray, one a Pharisee and the other a tax collector. The Pharisee stood by himself and prayed: "God, I thank you that I am not like other people—robbers, evildoers, adulterers—or even like this tax collector. I fast twice a week and give a tenth of all I get." But the tax collector stood at a distance. He would not even look up to heaven but beat his breast and said, "God, have mercy on me, a sinner." I tell you that this man, rather than the other, went home justified before God. For all those who exalt themselves will be humbled, and those who humble themselves will be exalted.'"*

Parable Narration: In this parable, Jesus addresses those who were confident in their self-righteousness and looked down on others. He tells the story of two men who went to the temple to pray. One was a Pharisee, known for his religious devotion, and the other a tax collector, often seen as a symbol of sin and corruption.

The Pharisee prayed proudly, listing his righteous deeds and comparing himself to others, including the tax collector. He claimed to fast twice a week and tithe on all his earnings. In contrast, the tax collector stood at a distance, would not even look up to heaven, and humbly beat his breast, confessing, "God, have mercy on me, a sinner."

Jesus concludes the parable by emphasizing that the tax collector, who humbled himself and recognized his need for God's mercy, went home justified before God, rather than the proud Pharisee. He adds that those who exalt themselves will be humbled, and those who humble themselves will be exalted.

Points to Reflect On:

- ✓ The parable contrasts the attitudes of self-righteousness and humility in prayer.
- ✓ It illustrates the importance of recognizing one's need for God's mercy and the danger of self-exaltation.
- ✓ The parable emphasizes that genuine righteousness comes from a humble heart.

Key Application: "The Parable of the Pharisee and the Publican" teaches us about the power of humility in prayer and the need to approach God with a contrite heart, acknowledging our dependence on His mercy. It warns against self-righteousness and pride.

Lessons in Our Life:

- ✓ Humility in Prayer: We should approach God in humility, acknowledging our need for His mercy, rather than comparing ourselves to others.
- ✓ Avoiding Self-Righteousness: The parable warns against self-righteousness and the temptation to exalt ourselves above others.
- ✓ True Righteousness: Genuine righteousness is not found in self-righteousness or comparing ourselves to others but in our relationship with God and our humble recognition of our need for His mercy.
- ✓ Exaltation through Humility: Those who humble themselves will be exalted by God,

while the proud will be humbled. Humility leads to a right relationship with God.

31. The Parable of the Leaven

Bible Verse: Matthew 13:33 *"He told them still another parable: 'The kingdom of heaven is like yeast that a woman took and mixed into about sixty pounds of flour until it worked all through the dough.'"*

Parable Narration: In this concise yet profound parable, Jesus describes the kingdom of heaven by likening it to yeast that a woman takes and mixes into a large amount of flour. The yeast works its way through the entire batch of dough.

While this parable is brief, it carries a significant message. The yeast, which represents the influence of the kingdom of heaven, starts as a small and hidden element but has the power to permeate and transform the entire batch of dough. It illustrates the transformative and pervasive nature of God's kingdom.

Points to Reflect On:

- ✓ The parable underscores the idea that the kingdom of heaven has a hidden yet transformative influence on individuals and society.
- ✓ It highlights the power of a small and seemingly insignificant element to bring about significant change.
- ✓ The parable encourages us to recognize the transformative work of God's kingdom in our lives and the world.

Key Application: "The Parable of the Leaven" teaches us about the transformative and pervasive influence of God's kingdom. It calls us to be open to this influence and to recognize the impact it can have on our lives and the world.

Lessons in Our Life:

- ✓ Hidden Influence: God's kingdom often works in ways that may not be immediately evident. It reminds us to be open to God's transformative work, even when it seems subtle.
- ✓ Small Beginnings: Just as yeast starts as a small element, great changes can begin with small, seemingly insignificant actions and decisions.
- ✓ Transformation: The parable encourages us to be open to the transformative power of God's kingdom in our lives, knowing that it can work through us to impact others and society.
- ✓ Awareness and Recognition: We should be aware of and recognize the work of God's kingdom in our lives and the lives of others, giving credit to the transformative influence of faith.

32. The Parable of the Unfinished Tower

Bible Verse: Luke 14:28-30 *"Suppose one of you wants to build a tower. Won't you first sit down and estimate the cost to see if you have enough money to complete it? For if you lay the foundation and are not able to finish it, everyone who sees it will ridicule you, saying, 'This person began to build and wasn't able to finish.'"*

Parable Narration: In this parable, Jesus provides a practical analogy to emphasize the importance of careful planning and commitment in discipleship. He uses the example of someone who intends to build a tower. Before starting the construction, Jesus suggests that the individual should first sit down and calculate the costs to ensure they have enough resources to complete the project.

The reason for this careful planning is clear: if the person lays the foundation but cannot finish the tower due to insufficient resources, they will face ridicule from others who will say, "This person began to build and wasn't able to finish."

Points to Reflect On:

- ✓ The parable highlights the significance of counting the cost before embarking on a significant task.
- ✓ It underscores the need for commitment and the ability to follow through on one's intentions and plans.
- ✓ The parable warns of the consequences of incomplete or unfulfilled commitments.

Key Application: "The Parable of the Unfinished Tower" teaches us about the importance of thoughtful planning, commitment, and the necessity of counting the cost in various aspects of life, including our walk with Christ. It reminds us to carefully consider our intentions and the resources required for the journey.

Lessons in Our Life:

- ✓ Counting the Cost: We are encouraged to carefully consider the demands and challenges of our commitments and to be prepared for the journey ahead.
- ✓ Commitment and Follow-Through: The parable emphasizes the significance of commitment and the ability to see our intentions through to completion.
- ✓ Avoiding Ridicule: It warns us of the potential consequences of making commitments without the resolve to fulfill them, which can lead to ridicule and disappointment.
- ✓ Wise Planning: The parable underscores the importance of wisdom in our decision-making and planning to avoid unnecessary setbacks.

33. The Parable of the Unfinished War

Bible Verse: Luke 14:31-33 *"Or suppose a king is about to go to war against another king. Won't he first sit down and consider whether he is able with ten thousand men to oppose the one coming against him with twenty thousand? If he is not able, he will send a delegation while the other is still a long way off and will ask for terms of peace. In the same way, those of you who do not give up everything you have cannot be my disciples."*

Parable Narration: In this parable, Jesus uses the analogy of a king preparing for war to convey a lesson about the cost of discipleship. He describes a situation where a king is about to go into battle against another king who has twice as many soldiers. Before engaging in the conflict, the king must assess whether his ten thousand soldiers can successfully oppose the approaching army of twenty thousand.

If the king realizes that he lacks the strength to win the battle, he chooses a different course of action. Instead of proceeding to fight a losing battle, he opts to send a delegation to the opposing king while the enemy is still a long way off. The purpose of this delegation is to negotiate terms of peace.

Following this parable, Jesus concludes by stating that those who do not give up everything they have cannot be His disciples. He is emphasizing the high cost and commitment required to follow Him.

Points to Reflect On:

- ✓ The parable illustrates the importance of considering the cost and potential challenges before committing to a significant endeavor.
- ✓ It highlights the wisdom of making peace arrangements rather than engaging in a costly and likely losing battle.
- ✓ The parable underscores the radical commitment and surrender required to be a true disciple of Christ.

Key Application: "The Parable of the Unfinished War" underscores the cost of discipleship and the need for wholehearted commitment to follow Christ. It encourages us to count the cost of being a disciple and to be willing to surrender everything for the sake of the kingdom.

Lessons in Our Life:

- ✓ Counting the Cost: We are called to consider the demands and sacrifices involved in discipleship before making the commitment.
- ✓ Wisdom in Surrender: The parable reminds us of the wisdom of surrendering to Christ and His lordship, avoiding unnecessary battles and losses.
- ✓ Wholehearted Commitment: To be a true disciple, we must be willing to give up everything for Christ and His kingdom.
- ✓ Peaceful Resolution: Just as the king in the parable seeks terms of peace to avoid a costly war, we should pursue peaceful resolutions in our relationships and conflicts.

34. The Parable of the Two Debtors

Bible Verse: Luke 7:41-43 *"Two people owed money to a certain moneylender. One owed him five hundred denarii, and the other fifty. Neither of them had the money to pay him back, so he forgave the debts of both. Now which of them will love him more?" Simon replied, 'I suppose the one who had the bigger debt forgiven.' 'You have judged correctly,' Jesus said."*

Parable Narration: In this parable, Jesus tells of two debtors who owed money to a moneylender. One debtor owed a substantial sum of five hundred denarii, while the other owed a smaller amount of fifty denarii. Neither of them had the means to repay their debts.

The moneylender, showing great mercy and grace, forgave the debts of both debtors entirely, relieving them of their financial burdens. Jesus then poses a question to Simon, who was hosting Him at the time, asking which of the two debtors would love the moneylender more. Simon correctly answers that it would be the one who had the bigger debt forgiven.

Points to Reflect On:

- ✓ The parable illustrates the profound concept of debt forgiveness and its impact on the hearts of those forgiven.
- ✓ It highlights the contrast between the two debtors and the depth of their gratitude and love for the moneylender.
- ✓ The parable emphasizes the transformative power of grace and forgiveness.

Key Application: "The Parable of the Two Debtors" teaches us about the transformative effect of grace and forgiveness in our lives. It reminds us of the depth of our gratitude and love when we understand the extent of our forgiveness.

Lessons in Our Life:

- ✓ Gratitude and Love: We are encouraged to reflect on the depth of our gratitude and love for God when we recognize the extent of our sins and the forgiveness we have received.
- ✓ Understanding Grace: The parable underscores the importance of understanding and appreciating God's grace and forgiveness in our lives.
- ✓ Compassion for Others: As recipients of grace and forgiveness, we are called to show compassion and forgiveness to others, recognizing that we too have been forgiven.
- ✓ Transformative Power: Forgiveness has the power to transform hearts and lives, leading to a profound change in our relationship with God.

35. The Parable of the Laborers in the Vineyard

Bible Verse: Matthew 20:1-16 *"For the kingdom of heaven is like a landowner who went out early in the morning to hire workers for his vineyard. He agreed to pay them a denarius for the day and sent them into his vineyard. About nine in the morning he went out and saw others standing in the marketplace doing nothing. He told them, 'You also go and work in my vineyard, and I will pay you whatever is right.' So they went. He went out again about noon and about three in the afternoon and did the same thing. About five in the afternoon, he went out and found still others standing around. He asked them, 'Why have you been standing here all day long doing nothing?' 'Because no one has hired us,' they answered. He said to them, 'You also go and work in my vineyard.' When evening came, the owner of the vineyard said to his foreman, 'Call the workers and pay them their wages, beginning with the last ones hired and going on to the first.' The workers who were hired about five in the afternoon came and each received a denarius. So when those came who were hired first, they expected to receive more. But each one of them also received a denarius. When they received it, they began to grumble against the landowner. 'These who were hired last worked only one hour,' they said, 'and you have made them equal to us who have borne the burden of the work and the heat of the day.' But he answered one of them, 'I am not being unfair to you, friend. Didn't you agree to work for a denarius? Take your pay and go. I want to give the one who was hired last the same as I gave you. Don't I have the right to do what I want with my* *own money? Or are you envious because I am generous?' So the last will be first, and the first will be last."*

Parable Narration: In this parable, Jesus describes the kingdom of heaven using a story of a landowner who hires laborers to work in his vineyard at various times during the day. He initially hires workers early in the morning and agrees to pay them a denarius for the day's work. Throughout the day, he hires additional laborers at different hours, promising to pay them what is right.

At the end of the day, when it's time to pay the laborers, the landowner instructs his foreman to start with the workers hired last and proceed to the first ones hired. Surprisingly, the workers hired last receive a denarius, just like those who worked the entire day. This leads the early workers to grumble, feeling that it's unfair. The landowner responds by stating that he has the right to be generous, and they had agreed to work for a denarius. He highlights that the last will be first, and the first will be last.

Points to Reflect On:

- ✓ The parable challenges our notions of fairness and generosity.
- ✓ It illustrates God's generosity and His right to bestow grace as He pleases.
- ✓ It conveys the idea that the kingdom of heaven operates on principles different from worldly expectations.

Key Application: "The Parable of the Laborers in the Vineyard" teaches us about God's abundant grace and generosity in His kingdom. It invites us to consider the ways in which we view and respond to

God's blessings and the blessings He bestows on others.

Lessons in Our Life:

- ✓ God's Generosity: The parable reminds us of God's generous nature and the abundance of His grace, which is not based on human merit.
- ✓ Avoiding Comparison: We are encouraged to avoid comparing ourselves to others in matters of God's grace, as it can lead to discontent and misunderstanding.
- ✓ Humility and Gratitude: We should approach God's blessings with humility and gratitude, recognizing that we all receive His grace freely.
- ✓ Kingdom Principles: The parable highlights that the kingdom of heaven operates on principles of grace and generosity that may differ from worldly standards.

36. The Parable of the Vine and Branches

Bible Verse: John 15:1-8 *"I am the true vine, and my Father is the gardener. He cuts off every branch in me that bears no fruit, while every branch that does bear fruit he prunes so that it will be even more fruitful. You are already clean because of the word I have spoken to you. Remain in me, and I will remain in you. No branch can bear fruit by itself; it must remain in the vine. Neither can you bear fruit unless you remain in me. I am the vine; you are the branches. If a man remains in me and I in him, he will bear much fruit; apart from me you can do nothing. If anyone does not remain in me, he is like a branch that is thrown away and withers; such branches are picked up, thrown into the fire and burned. If you remain in me and my words remain in you, ask whatever you wish, and it will be given you. This is to my Father's glory, that you bear much fruit, showing yourselves to be my disciples."*

Parable Narration: In this parable, Jesus uses the metaphor of a vine and branches to illustrate the intimate connection between Him and His followers. He declares Himself as the true vine, and God the Father as the gardener who tends to the vineyard.
Jesus explains that every branch in Him that bears no fruit is cut off, while those that do bear fruit are pruned to become even more fruitful. He emphasizes the necessity of remaining in Him, just as branches remain attached to the vine to bear fruit. He underscores the idea that apart from Him, we can do nothing.

The parable describes the consequences of not remaining in Him, comparing those who do not remain in Him to withered branches that are eventually thrown into the fire. On the other hand, those who remain in Him and have His words abiding in them are promised that their requests will be granted, and they will bear much fruit, glorifying God and showing themselves to be His disciples.

Points to Reflect On:

- ✓ The parable highlights the vital connection between Jesus as the vine and His followers as the branches.
- ✓ It emphasizes the significance of bearing fruit and the process of pruning for greater fruitfulness.
- ✓ The parable underscores that apart from Christ, we can do nothing of lasting significance.

Key Application: "The Parable of the Vine and Branches" teaches us about the necessity of abiding in Christ and maintaining a close, intimate relationship with Him. It encourages us to focus on bearing fruit and seeking God's glory in all that we do.

Lessons in Our Life:

- ✓ Abiding in Christ: We are called to remain closely connected to Jesus in all aspects of our lives, seeking His guidance and strength.
- ✓ Fruitfulness: The parable challenges us to bear fruit in our faith and actions, with the understanding that God desires our spiritual growth and effectiveness.
- ✓ Pruning and Growth: Just as branches are pruned for greater fruitfulness, we should be

open to God's refining work in our lives, even in times of trials and difficulties.

- ✓ Dependence on Christ: We are reminded of our complete dependence on Christ, as apart from Him, we can achieve nothing of eternal significance.

37. The Parable of the New Cloth

Bible Verse: Matthew 9:16 *"No one sews a patch of unshrunk cloth on an old garment, for the patch will pull away from the garment, making the tear worse."*

Parable Narration: In this concise parable, Jesus uses the analogy of sewing a new patch of unshrunk cloth on an old garment. He points out that no one would attempt to do this, as the new cloth, when it shrinks, would pull away from the old garment, creating a worse tear.

Points to Reflect On:

- ✓ The parable illustrates the impracticality of combining new and old materials that don't align or adapt well.
- ✓ It highlights the importance of considering compatibility when making changes or additions.

Key Application: "The Parable of the New Cloth" reminds us to consider compatibility and the need for wisdom when introducing new ideas, practices, or beliefs into established systems or traditions. It underscores the importance of thoughtful, harmonious integration.

Lessons in Our Life:

- ✓ Compatibility: We should be mindful of the compatibility of new concepts or practices with existing ones, to avoid conflict and disharmony.
- ✓ Wisdom in Change: The parable emphasizes the need for wisdom and discernment when making changes within established structures or belief systems.

- ✓ Respect for Tradition: We should appreciate the value of traditions and established practices, while also recognizing the potential for growth and adaptation.
- ✓ Balancing Innovation: Innovation and tradition can coexist when introduced thoughtfully and with an understanding of their impact.

38. The Parable of the New Wine

Bible Verse: Matthew 9:17 *"Neither do people pour new wine into old wineskins. If they do, the skins will burst; the wine will run out and the wineskins will be ruined. No, they pour new wine into new wineskins, and both are preserved."*

Parable Narration: In this parable, Jesus uses the analogy of new wine and wineskins to convey a valuable lesson. He explains that pouring new wine into old wineskins is not advisable because as the new wine ferments and expands, it would stretch the old, rigid wineskins beyond their capacity. This would lead to the bursting of the old wineskins, causing the wine to spill and the wineskins to be ruined. Instead, Jesus advises that new wine should be poured into new wineskins so that both the wine and the wineskins are preserved.

Points to Reflect On:

- ✓ The parable underscores the incompatibility of new and old systems or beliefs when they don't align or adapt.
- ✓ It highlights the importance of using appropriate vessels for new and dynamic concepts or practices.

Key Application: "The Parable of the New Wine" encourages us to consider the compatibility and receptiveness of the containers, or "vessels," that hold new ideas, teachings, or practices. It emphasizes the need for adaptability and innovation in our approach.

Lessons in Our Life:

- ✓ Adaptability: We are reminded of the importance of adapting to new ideas and changes, especially in our spiritual journey, to avoid rigidity and stagnation.
- ✓ Innovation: The parable encourages us to embrace innovation and fresh perspectives, while also being mindful of the means by which they are introduced.
- ✓ Preservation of Traditions: We should balance the introduction of new concepts with the preservation of valuable traditions and teachings.
- ✓ Choosing the Right Vessels: The parable illustrates the significance of choosing the right containers or methods for presenting and accommodating new, dynamic principles.

39. The Parable of the Strong Man

Bible Verse: Matthew 12:29 *"Or again, how can anyone enter a strong man's house and carry off his possessions unless he first ties up the strong man? Then he can plunder his house."*

Parable Narration: In this brief but profound parable, Jesus presents the analogy of a strong man's house. He asks how it would be possible for anyone to enter the house of a strong man and take away his possessions unless the strong man is first bound or tied up. It's a simple yet powerful illustration.

Points to Reflect On:

- ✓ The parable highlights the need to overcome resistance and obstacles in order to achieve a goal.
- ✓ It suggests that prevailing over a strong opponent requires strategic action.

Key Application: "The Parable of the Strong Man" prompts us to consider the concept of overcoming resistance, obstacles, or opposition to achieve a greater purpose. It emphasizes the importance of strategic planning and action in the face of challenges.

Lessons in Our Life:

- ✓ Overcoming Challenges: We are reminded that overcoming formidable challenges often requires careful planning and strategic efforts.
- ✓ Persistence: The parable encourages persistence in the pursuit of our goals, even when faced with strong opposition.

- ✓ Preparation: It underscores the significance of being prepared and equipped for the challenges we may encounter in life.
- ✓ Spiritual Significance: The parable can also be applied to spiritual matters, emphasizing the need to confront and overcome spiritual obstacles and strongholds in our lives.

40.The Parable of the Lamp on a Stand

Bible Verse: Mark 4:21 *"He said to them, 'Do you bring in a lamp to put it under a bowl or a bed? Instead, don't you put it on its stand?'"*

Parable Narration: In this concise parable, Jesus draws upon the everyday practice of using a lamp. He questions whether someone would light a lamp and then hide it under a bowl or a bed. Instead, the natural inclination is to place the lamp on its stand so that it illuminates the room and provides light to all who are present.

Points to Reflect On:

- ✓ The parable emphasizes the purpose of a lamp, which is to provide light and illumination.
- ✓ It questions the idea of hiding something that is meant to bring clarity and understanding.

Key Application: "The Parable of the Lamp on a Stand" encourages us to consider the purpose of our actions and the message we convey. It calls for transparency and the sharing of knowledge, rather than concealing or obscuring it.

Lessons in Our Life:

- ✓ Sharing Knowledge: We are prompted to share our knowledge, wisdom, and insights with others for their benefit.
- ✓ Transparency: The parable advocates for transparency and openness in our actions and communication.
- ✓ Purposeful Living: It encourages us to live with purpose and to let our light shine, rather than keeping it hidden.

- ✓ Spiritual Significance: The parable has spiritual implications, encouraging us to share the light of faith and truth with others.

Conclusion

In the rich tapestry of the Bible's teachings, the parables of Jesus stand as shining gems of wisdom and insight. Each one is a lantern that casts light on the path of our spiritual journey, revealing profound truths that continue to echo across time and touch the very essence of our humanity.

As we come to the end of **'Parables of Jesus for a Meaningful Life: *Walking in the Master Teacher's Footsteps!'*** we have traversed the diverse landscape of these timeless stories, each offering a unique glimpse into the heart of Jesus' teachings. From the Good Samaritan's call to compassion, to the prodigal son's tale of redemption, and the mustard seed's lesson in faith, we have delved into a world of wisdom that transcends cultures, religions, and generations.

These parables, though ancient, remain evergreen in their ability to guide us in our modern lives. They challenge us to love unconditionally, to show mercy and forgiveness, and to live with integrity and purpose. In the midst of a tumultuous world, they remind us that there is a greater purpose, a higher calling, and an eternal love that accompanies us on our journey.

But the power of these parables extends beyond the pages of a book. It lives in the way we apply these lessons to our daily lives. It's in the kindness we show to strangers, the forgiveness we offer to those who have wronged us, and the patience we practice when facing challenges. The true essence of these parables is not just in understanding them but in embodying their teachings.

As we conclude this book, we invite you to carry the light of these parables forward. Let them be a source of inspiration when you face adversity, a compass for moral decision-making, and a reminder of the boundless grace available to all. Their wisdom is a gift that keeps on giving, enabling us to navigate the complexities of life with courage, grace, and love.

May you find meaning and purpose in the teachings of Jesus' parables and continue to share their wisdom with those you encounter on your journey. For in doing so, you become a living testament to the enduring power of these stories and the transformative message they carry.

Our hope is that this book has deepened your understanding of the parables and, more importantly, has ignited a desire to live them out. Just as a lamp is meant to be placed on a stand to illuminate the room, may you be a beacon of light in a world that often seems shadowed by darkness.

Thank you for joining us on this enlightening journey through the world of parables. As you move forward, may the lessons you've encountered here be a source of strength, comfort, and inspiration.

About the Author 'GERARD ASSEY'

Gerard Assey is a Graduate in Economics, a PGD in Management (HRD) and holds a Doctorate in Leadership. Gerard holds several International Qualifications in Sales, Debt Collection, Training & Teaching, and is a 'Fellow' of the prestigious 'Institute of Sales & Marketing Management'-UK, a Certified NLP Practitioner, a 'Certified Trainer', an 'Accredited Management Teacher-Behavioral Sciences', a 'Certified Competency Facilitator', a 'Certified Management Consultant'- (the International credentials of a professional management consultant, awarded in accordance with global standards of the ICMCI); and a Certification from the University of Michigan in 'Successful Negotiation: Essential Strategies and Skills'

He is also a Member of the 'National Association of Sales Professionals' backed with several years experience in varied industries, both in India and Overseas. He also holds an 'Etiquette Consultant' Certification from the USA (by Sue Fox, Author of Best Seller: 'Business Etiquette for Dummies'. She has trained some of the top celebrities' world over). He was also a recipient of a scholarship for extensive training in Japan on 'Corporate Management for India'.

Gerard Assey is 'Founder & Chief Corporate Trainer' of the Group: '**Citius, Altius, Fortius Unlimited**'- an organization that **celebrated 20 years of Glorious Service** in 2021, focusing on 3 Core Competencies:

People. Performance. Profit; in functional areas of Sales & Marketing, HR & Organizational Development, covering Recruitment, Training & Consultancy!

Having managed organizations with large Sales Forces in India & Overseas, his specialization cover extensive areas of Sales Training (All levels - Presentation, Negotiation, Key/ Strategic Accounts Management & Managerial Skills for all sectors), Bid Proposal/ Capture Planning/ Management Trainings, Retail Sales, Customer Service & Customer Retention Programs, Training for Prevention & Collection of Debt, Self & Personal Development Programs (Time Management, Teamwork & Team Building, Business Etiquette & Personal Grooming, Leadership & Managerial Skills, People Management Skills, Train-the-Trainer etc), including preparation of Custom-designed Business Manuals for Internal (HR, Induction, and Sales etc) & External use (Instruction, User Manuals).

Gerard has successfully conducted over 6000 Trainings & Workshops (as of Nov '23) all across India, Middle East, Africa, Europe & S.E. Asia. Besides public programs conducted regularly, both in India & Overseas, he has some of the top names as clients whom he services from Single Owners to large Public & Government undertakings, covering all sectors, for their in-house needs.

His website: www.CollectionSkills.com is the only one in this part of the world to be featured in the 'Collections & Credit Risk Magazine-USA' under 'Who's Who in Training' and ranks TOP, along with other websites listed below on most search engines.

Gerard is author of 96 books already (Nov 2023),

A few of our business related books:

1. Bite-sized Bits on Commonsense Management
2. Heart to Heart on Life's Principles'
3. How to become a Successful Manager
4. The Sales Professionals' Master Workbook of S.Y.S.T.E.M.S
5. The Professional Business Email Etiquette Handbook & Guide
6. The Professional Business Video-Conferencing Etiquette Handbook & Guide
7. Professional Presentation Skills
8. Exceptional Customer Service
9. Professional Tele-Marketing Skills
10. Professional Debt Collection Skills
11. The G.R.E.A.T. Sales & Service Workbook
12. Sales Training Advantage for Results (*The Ultimate Sales Training Manual to enable you stand out as a S.T.A.R.*)
13. CEO Daily Planner & Organizer
14. The Sales Professionals' Master Daily Planner
15. The Professional Debt Collector's Master Daily Planner
16. My Daily Planner & Organizer
17. MY EMERGENCY INFORMATION RECORD (Family Emergency & Peace of Mind Planner)
18. The Ultimate Therapist & Counselors Planner and Organizer
19. Building an Ethical Workplace
20. Managing Relationships at Work
21. Managing Business Meetings Effectively
22. Effective Delegation Skills
23. Goal Setting for Success
24. B2B Selling by Email
25. Professional Business Etiquette & Grooming
26. Dining Etiquette & Table Manners
27. Effective Networking Skills
28. Grooming, Etiquette & Manners for Teens, Young Adults & Future Leaders
29. Inter-Personal Skills
30. Get Ready, Get Hired!
31. Selling in a Recession
32. Effective Receivables Management in an Economic Downturn!
33. Real Estate & Property Sales Training
34. Credit Sales & Accounts Receivable Management
35. Selling Skills for Real Estate & Property Advisors
36. Take G.R.E.A.T. C.A.R.E!

37. Spa, Salon & Health Club Selling Skills
38. Selling Travel, Holiday & MICE Services
39. Selling Skills for Spa's, Salons & Health Clubs
40. Retailing in Salons & Spas
41. Selling Holiday, Vacation, Tours & Packages
42. The Power of Sales Referrals
43. Selling Luxury
44. Technical Selling Skills
45. Financial Advisors Sales Training
46. Dealing with Burnout at Work Monopolize Your Markets
47. Selling to Affluent Customers
48. Growing up with Grace
49. Financial Selling Skills
50. *The Effective Manager's Guide: Key Skills to Thrive*
51. From Aspiring to Inspiring: A Guide for New Managers on the Rise
52. The Power of Focus
53. Selling with Integrity: Sell Like Jesus The Perfect Role Model!
54. 31 Habits of Champions: Your 31-Day Journey to Greatness
55. Rejecting Grasshopper Talk: From Grasshopper to Giant-Killer-*Defeating Giants Daily!*
56. Navigate the AI-Powered Future of Bid & Proposals: Up-Skill to Stay Relevant with Alternative Career Paths & Opportunities
57. Hiring Sales Winners
58. Present with Impact
59. Success Unlocked: *Breaking Free from Habits that Hold You Back*
60. Complaints to Cheers, Feedback to Gold: Mastering Complaints Management
61. Thriving Together: *Cultivating Diversity, Equity, and Inclusion*
62. Coaching Skills for Sales Managers
63. Soaring to Success in Business & Leadership: Swifter, Higher, Stronger!
64. From Classroom to Podium: A Student's Guide to Powerful Public Speaking & Presentation Skills
65. Developing Self-Discipline
66. The CEO's 31-Day Power Plan: Unlocking Success through Essential Traits
67. Credibility Matters

...And some of his most recent Christian Books being:

1. A Bouquet of Praises for My KING
2. Christian Jokes for the Serious Religious' Folks!
3. Jesus Healed You!
4. Praise24Ever! (also in Tamil version)
5. The 5G Network of GOD
6. Building Faith over F.E.A.R- FACE EVERYTHING AND RISE with JESUS
7. Hebrew and Greek Praise and Worship Words
8. Godly Mothers' and Grandmothers' Bible Story time for Kids!
9. Miracles of Jesus in Pictures
10. Raise your Praise all 365 Days
11. Thanking GOD with an Attitude of Gratitude
12. Meditating on the Attributes of GOD
13. Puppet Scripts
14. Alcohol Ruins, JESUS Reforms, Renews & Restores!
15. Habakkuk 2:2 Christian Daily Journal, Planner & Organizer
16. ABC of GOD's Word for Handwriting Practice
17. Daily Bible Verse Handwriting Practice (Building Godly Character & Faith through Cursive Handwriting Practice!)
18. Guiding Light: Fun & Faith-Building Bible Activities for Children
19. Rejecting Grasshopper Talk: From Grasshopper to Giant-Killer-*Defeating Giants Daily!*
20. Teen Titans of Faith: *Building Courage, Determination & Christ-like-Esteem*
21. I AM Empowered: *Unleashing Divine Power with Positive Declarations*
22. Be A Solution Provider-*From Passion to Purpose*: *A Biblical Guide to Being the Answer to the World!*
23. Miracles of JESUS
24. Parables of Jesus for a Meaningful Life!

Besides regularly contributing to business & trade journals, including international ones such as the 'Creative Training Techniques' and the 'Sales News' of the U.S.A, He is also a member of several prestigious bodies & trade associations, having participated in many Conferences & Workshops in India & Overseas.
Prior to his last assignment of leading & managing a large MNC as head, Gerard had a 3-year stint in the Middle East as a Consultant with a leading British Consultancy Firm.

As the past 'Official Country Representative' for the International Business Award- 'THE STEVIES'-(the business world's own Oscar) for about 4 years- he ensured a few Indian companies that qualify for the same every year!

Gerard can be contacted at:
Email: training@Sales-Training.in,training@CollectionSkills.com
Websites:

www.Sales-Training.in
www.EtiquetteWorks.in
www.CollectionSkills.com
www.RetailSalesTraining.in
www.SalesTrainingIndia.com
www.ManualPreparation.com
www.TrainingWithPuppets.com
www.FirstContactAcademy.com
www.SalesAndMarketingRecruiter.com

Our TRAININGS & BOOKS that can help your team

- ✓ **Sales Effectiveness**: Selling Skills for any Sector: Service/ Logistics/ FMCG Realty/ Insurance & Finance/ Media/ SPA's, Health Clubs & Salons/ Key Account Management, Effective Negotiation Skills/ Bid & Proposal Management Skills/ Retail Sales Training: Any Sector (Auto, Jewelry, Clothing, Luxury etc)
- ✓ **Customer Service Skills**-Complaints Handling & Customer Retention
- ✓ **Debt Prevention & Collection Skills**
- ✓ **Etiquette & Grooming**
- ✓ **Leadership & Managerial Skills**
- ✓ **Self & Personal Development Skills**: Presentation Skills/ Effective Communication Skills/Business Proposal Writing Skills/ Problem Solving & Decision Making Skills/ Empowering Secretaries-The perfect PA! (For Secretaries & PA's)/ Effective Time Management/ Teamwork & Teambuilding/ P.R.I.D.E- **P**ersonal **R**esponsibility **I**n **D**elivering **E**xcellence

www.ingramcontent.com/pod-product-compliance
Lightning Source LLC
LaVergne TN
LVHW010113170826
845678LV00012B/2383

* 9 7 8 8 1 9 6 5 8 0 7 4 2 *